IT IS FINISHED!

Patricia Marlett

It Is Finished!
Copyright © 2018, 2022 by Patricia Marlett
All rights reserved.

No part of this publication may be reproduced, stored in a retrieval system or transmitted in any way by any means, electronic, mechanical, photocopy, recording or otherwise without the prior permission of the author except as provided by USA copyright law.

Scriptures from the King James Bible
Published in the United States of America
Published by High Tower Publishing

First Edition - 2018   ISBN: 978-0-9994680-4-3
Second Edition - 2022   ISBN: 978-0-9994680-4-3

High Tower Publishing
2 Samuel 22:3

Acknowledgement

I will always, and forevermore, acknowledge and give thanks to God. I honor, praise and give the glory to my heavenly Father; for it is by His grace, that I am blessed. He is my inspiration and with the gift He has bestowed upon me, I write in His honor to glorify His name.

Also, deep appreciation to my husband, Mark, for his unwavering love, support, and dedication as I pursue my passion. You are my rock, I love you.

Dedication

This book is dedicated to all who seek
a relationship in Christ with the Father.

*Jesus saith unto him,
I am the way, the truth, and the life:
no man cometh unto the Father, but by me.*
John 14:6

TABLE OF CONTENT

Note from the Author _____ 11

Preface _____ 14

Chapter One: The Foundation _____ 19

Chapter Two: The Adam's _____ 27

Chapter Three: The Son _____ 39

Chapter Four: The Righteousness _____ 45

Chapter Five: The Rest _____ 50

Chapter Six: The Choice _____ 56

Summary _____ 61

Seven Final Words of Christ on the Cross _____ 67

The Trinity in Christ _____ 69

Names of Jesus Christ _____ 80

Excerpt: Fervent Prayer _____ 99

Excerpt: Children in the Crossfire _____ 101

Excerpt: Everlasting Love, God's Greatest Gift ___ 103

NOTE FROM THE AUTHOR

*If any man speak, let him speak as the oracles
of God; if any man minister, let him do it as of
the ability which God giveth: that God in all things
may be glorified through Jesus Christ, to whom
be praise and dominion for ever and ever. Amen.*
Peter 4:11

It is with honor and glory to our heavenly Father that I take great pleasure in presenting this book to share the truth of God's Word as taught in the Scriptures, and to assure each person who reads the content on the following pages that everything God created was meant for you.

It has always been about you when God established the foundation of His Creation as we read in the Bible and continues throughout eternity. I hope you gain insight of how much you are truly loved, and how desirous the Father is for you to be with Him in spirit, today and forever.

God made all things possible through His Son, Jesus, when He gave man a new and better covenant. As a beneficiary of this testament, we have the free will to personally decide if we want a life with Him, one that is eternal. Though it is by our choice, God wants all His children to come home to the Kingdom of Heaven.

We can be with our Father this very moment, spiritually, if we become one in spirit with His Son. The first step is a desire to have a relationship with God and become a spirit-born child of the Father. In Christ, we are changed from sinner to saint and secured as a joint-heir in the Kingdom.

I pray you are inspired to seek God and accept His Word as the very foundation of your life and maintain a relationship with your heavenly Father. Not simply know of Him, but fall in love with Him, learn His nature and understand what He has done for you, and what He gives to you, His child.

As a child to the parent, we should want our Father's love and a close bond with Him more than anything, ever. Only God can heal a broken body whether it is physical or emotional, only God can supply for personal and professional prosperity, and only God can give us eternal life. There is absolutely nothing permanent on this planet as this earthen place will one day be made anew to receive the New Jerusalem which will be the eternal home of every believer.

God's love, mercy, and grace are forever present and He will always protect and provide for His children. We are His most precious creation, made in His likeness, for His pleasure, never forgotten or forsaken. Promises, blessings, gifts, and power are within His Kingdom, and we are personally responsible to acquire the knowledge that God has set forth in His Word, so that we may partake of these heavenly treasures. Learn of the plans God has for your earthen life from the foundation of His Creation to the finished work of Christ on the Cross.

It is essential to understand the role of Christ as the Son of God and Son of Man in fulfilling the Father's plan. In Christ, we are given the gift of the Holy Spirit as our tutor and advocate in the Kingdom. The power of God comes through the Holy Spirit, the *Spirit of Truth*. This is crucial to living in the spirit and receiving what has been prepared for you.

There will appear a redundancy within this book, for when speaking of God, the Son, and the Holy Spirit, all are God; and yet, He presents Himself as separate personages for man's purpose. Therefore, there may be a repetitive thought in expressing the importance of God and His Kingdom of Heaven. However, a conscious effort has been made to keep the redundancy to a minimum.

With forethought, there are Scriptures appropriately placed to serve as a reference to what God's Word says as the focus is always on His truth. The Scriptures may be applicable more than once.

Our relationship with our heavenly Father is defined in our belief, trust, and unwavering faith. We are not lost souls wandering aimlessly throughout this life, but saints made righteous in Christ for the Father.

PREFACE

*For God so loved the world, that he gave
his only begotten Son, that whosoever believeth in
him should not perish, but have everlasting life.*
John 3:16

It Is Finished! is about coming to the end of our sinful self and picking up the Cross of Christ. What God and the Word created at the foundation, the Son fulfills on the Cross; therefore, from Creation to Cross the plans God has for man will be manifested in those who accept their position in Christ. We have a place in the Kingdom of Heaven because of what God desired and the Son accomplished; fulfilling the plan of God.

It is a transformation from sinner to saint, to living a spirit life in Christ governed by the principles of the Kingdom of Heaven, and accepting the Word of God as the very element of life. The Father and the Son have provided everything man will ever need in this earthen lifetime, and eternally.

Our spirit is awakened when we accept Christ, for our spirit is of His Spirit. We are born of the Spirit of God and live by His Word that our relationship is strengthened as we mature in the knowledge of Him. It is living righteous in Christ.

God in the personages of the Father, the Son, and the Holy Spirit is for the purpose of giving to you, serving you, protecting and providing for you. Notice the Father <u>gives</u>, the Son <u>serves</u>, and the Holy Spirit <u>provides</u>. It is important to know the role of Christ as the Son of God on the throne, and the Son of Man on the Cross. To obtain authority and supernatural power that is given to every person born of the Son of God, it begins with Christ.

It is our responsibility to learn the Kingdom precepts, so that we are able to position ourselves to receive what the Father and the Son have planned and finished. Once born of Christ's Spirit, we acknowledge the gift of the Holy Spirit, who is the Spirit of God, the *Spirit of Truth*. As God provides through grace, it is our faith that releases the Kingdom power. God supplies the grace and we furnish the faith, for they go together like a hand in a glove.

All the Father's blessings are continuously flowing like water over a waterfall; however, if we don't put a bucket underneath to capture the water, we remain without. We receive through faith. *But without faith it is impossible to please him: for he that cometh to God must believe that he is, and that he is a rewarder of them that diligently seek him.* Hebrews 11:6

Without the understanding of how God established His Kingdom and what Christ fulfilled on the Cross, we can be remiss in receiving the promises. The Father and the Son have finished their work, and now we should desire to live in the Kingdom as a spirit person in Christ.

IT IS FINISHED!

Therefore we are buried with him by baptism into death: that like as Christ was raised up from the dead by the glory of the Father, even so we also should walk in newness of life.
Romans 6:4

CHAPTER ONE

THE FOUNDATION

*When Jesus therefore had received the vinegar,
he said, It is finished: and he bowed his head,
and gave up the ghost.*
John 19:30

Christ's final words on the Cross before He released His Spirit were: *It is Finished!* In nearly two-thousand years, what is the significance of these three omnipotent words in our life today? The answer is everything. When Jesus hung on the Cross at Golgotha, just outside the gates of Jerusalem, all that was planned during the seven days of God's Creation was declared finished. *For by him were all things created, that are in heaven, and that are in earth, visible and invisible, whether they be thrones, or dominions, or principalities, or powers: all things were created by him, and for him: And he is before all things, and by him all things consist.* Colossians 1:16-17

It was four-thousand years from the finished work of God in the beginning for Christ to hang on a piece of wood and proclaim the work of the Father is finished. It came full circle from Creation to Cross; God declaring it and the Son fulfilling the plans God had for man.

The Kingdom of Heaven and Earth was established prior to Adam. On the sixth day of God's Creation, He formed man from the dirt of the earth and breathed His Spirit into him creating man with a body, soul, and spirit. *And the Lord God formed man of the dust of the ground, and breathed into his nostrils the breath of life; and man became a living soul*. Genesis 2:7 Man was named from the very place he came from which in Hebrew *Adamah* means earth; however, the English translation is *Adam*. God created Adam and Eve to be His children. They were spirit persons of His Spirit within a physical body.

Why is this important to you? Because what God spoke and the Word manifested has come to fruition in preparing an eternal life to those who believe. Once man was created, the first Adam, generations followed; however, it required the second Adam, Christ, to fulfill God's plan.

Adam brought carnality upon man through sin with his disobedience to God, while the second Adam redeems man of sin. As Adam was a spirit person living in the Garden of Eden, so are we born a spirit person in Christ as it was in the Garden. Without this happening, man would not exist for sin would be the death of mankind.

Therefore, everything in the following generations as depicted in both the Old and New Testaments is about the redemption of man and is only possible because of the Word becoming flesh for man's sake. God left His throne as the second person of the Trinity and became the Son of Man and dwelt among men to reclaim the children lost through sin. *But made himself of no reputation, and took upon him the form of a servant, and was <u>made in the likeness of men</u>: And being found in fashion as a man, he humbled himself, and became obedient unto death, even the death of the cross.* Philippians 2:7-8

In the Old Testament, there is the celebration of Yeshua shown in the seven feasts with the Jews honoring the Messiah as a *shadow of things to come,* until the Word is born of flesh; a man living among the people. Though Jesus is reflected throughout the Old Testament, we relate to Him as Christ in the New Testament.

What does this have to do with you? The very same it had to do with the Israelites. In those words, *It is Finished*, is your beginning, literally. The work has been completed like an artist painting a masterpiece, and we are the recipients of all that God planned and Christ fulfilled. It is the beginning of our eternal life in the Kingdom of Heaven where peace, joy, and harmony is an unconditional lifestyle. A life whereby love is the very essence of our existence. However, this is not only a future event in the New Jerusalem, but a life that begins the day you are born of the Spirit of Christ for the Spirit Kingdom of God.

It is far more than believing Christ is the Son of God, but living it as your reality knowing He is within you. You are a new spirit person born of the second Adam for the Father as it was with the first Adam in the Garden of Eden. *Therefore if any man be in Christ, he is a new creature: old things are passed away; behold, all things are become new.* 2 Corinthians 5:17 Your old sinful self has died on the Cross, and you are sanctified by the blood of

Christ to be a child of the Almighty King, our Most High God.

The sinful nature of your natural life has been put to death on the Cross, so in newness of your spirit life you have the promises of the Father. To know how to receive what God and the Son have given requires under-standing what Christ's death represents as the Son of Man.

How do we obtain something we cannot see? First, we have to believe that it does exist and this is done through faith; trusting in the intangible, not visible to the eye. For example, we know of oxygen; however, we cannot see it but without it we wouldn't be here. We understand radio waves and electricity to run our de-vices and appliances, but we can't see them; and yet, we easily accept their existence.

God's Kingdom functions on His Word. Today, we have authority in the Word through His Son which is why we ask on the authority of Christ's name. *And whatsoever <u>ye shall ask in my name</u>, that will I do, that the Father may be glorified in the Son. If ye shall ask any thing in my name, I will do it.* John 14:13-14

When we abide by His Word, we will experience the promises such as healing, miracles, and prosperity; pro-visions for our life. *My son, <u>attend to my words</u>; incline thine ear unto my sayings. Let them not depart from thine eyes; keep them in the midst of thine heart. For they are life unto those that find them, and health to all their flesh. Keep thy heart with all diligence; <u>for out of it are the issues of life</u>.* Proverbs 4:20-23 It requires believing the things that are invisible to be more real than what we experience through our senses. We acknowledge God's truth over anything the earthen world reveals. For many, this is a tall leap of faith but that is exactly what faith is, believing in what you can't validate with the typical worldly measures.

God's world isn't meant to blend into our earthen one, but rather we are to step out of the natural by renewing our mind to the spirit realm. *And be not conformed to this world: but be ye transformed by the <u>renewing of your mind</u>, that ye may prove what is that good, and acceptable, and perfect, will of God.* Romans 12:2 Know the precepts of the Kingdom, so that your thoughts and decisions are based on truth; thereby, relying on the *Spirit of Truth* to teach you.

What makes the spirit world different? If you believe in God, then you could conclude that He has a home, the Kingdom of Heaven. If you believe in His Son who made it possible to be a child of God, then presumably you want the privilege of living within the Kingdom, especially when it is offered to you now. There can only be one reason anyone would refuse and that is because they don't accept Christ as their Lord and Savior; they don't believe.

However, for the believer, you have gained entrance into a spiritual world with wonders you can only desire to imagine. God and the Word became the Father and the Son *to* you and *for* you. You are given access to the Kingdom, spiritually, if you accept what Christ did when He took your place on the Cross.

Christ's purpose on earth was to return the lost children to the Father. He is the *Good Shepherd* who gathered the flock and taught of the Father and His Kingdom to all who gathered to hear Him. He is also the sacrificial *Lamb of God. Christ hath redeemed us from the curse of the law, being made a curse for us: for it is written, Cursed is every one that hangeth on a tree: That the blessing of Abraham might come on the Gentiles through Jesus Christ; that we might receive the promise of the Spirit through faith.* Galatians 3:13-14 In Christ, we are sanctified for the Father.

Christ gives you passage into the Kingdom of Heaven. Can it be this simple? Absolutely. It is man who complicates the things he doesn't understand. We create a chasm between God and ourselves with our self-righteousness. *Jesus saith unto him, I am the way, the truth, and the life: no man cometh unto the Father, but by me.* John 14:6 Only the righteousness of Christ makes us worthy to be in the Kingdom of God.

It was all done for you, for it has always been about you before you were conceived in your mother's womb. God has a plan for your earthen life and wants you to live it, to trust in Him. We begin by accepting what we cannot see to be more real than what the natural conveys. We search for the essence of the Kingdom by not being drawn to the earthen things, for they are temporal. There is nothing of this natural world that is permanent.

As children of God, we yearn for the intimacy of a relationship with our heavenly Father because we are connected in spirit. We know our true home, today and forever, is within His Kingdom.

How does all this manifest into your earthen life? It requires gaining knowledge of how the Spirit Kingdom functions and rely on the tutor God has given to you. All gifts and supernatural power come into our life through the Holy Spirit, our teacher and advocate.

We have witnessed this to be true with Jesus. He performed no miracles or healing until He was baptized with the Holy Spirit at Jordan. If He required the Holy Spirit, and His disciples were sent forth with the Holy

Spirit to continue Christ's ministry of the Kingdom, it is no different for us, today.

Though you are born into the Kingdom, have a covenant with the Son, and privileges to the spiritual treasures, you can abort it all even in your belief. If not practicing the truth of God's Word, belief can become tainted with unbelief; unbelief negates belief. Nothing is being withheld by the Father or the Son; however, belief, or lack thereof, denotes the outcome.

God's blessings flow through grace, and grace is forever present. God's Kingdom functions on mercy, grace, and faith. God's provision is mercy and grace and our part is faith. It is our faith that releases the blessings through grace. Therefore, there is no combining the spiritual and natural worlds. Like oil and water, they don't mix because one world is of God and the other, the earthen, is under the rule of Satan.

So how do we receive what the Father promised? The answer is our position in Christ. It is living our new birthright of the Son's Spirit with faith in the Word of God. We place our trust in the finished work of Christ.

Recalling the story Jesus told to His disciples of the father with two sons and their inheritance is an analogy of our relationship with our heavenly Father and what He desires to give to His children. In the story, the father loved both sons equally as revealed when the prodigal son returned home after having squandered his inheritance and the father ran to him; hugged and kissed him. The father gave him gifts and celebrated his return, for he never stopped loving his son even when he strayed.

The older son who remained and worked beside his father spoke angrily, claiming an injustice had been done to him. What did the father say to his elder son?

And he said unto him, Son, thou art ever with me, and all that I have is thine. Luke 15:31 Everything the father owned belonged to both his sons, but the oldest son didn't accept the unconditional love of his father. The elder son believed he needed to work and earn his father's love, so when the younger brother was dis-obedient, disrespectful, and undeserving of coming back into the family, the elder son rebelled with anger and resentment. The elder son's inheritance was there for him to take at anytime, but he didn't realize it be-cause he didn't see the father's love. In reality by His behavior, he was a prodigal son also.

There is no favoritism with God for He loves all His children. *For there is no respect of persons with God.* Romans 2:11 This is where many believers are today. We aren't aware of our heavenly Father's love; and thus, aren't receiving the inheritance that is ours for the asking. The younger son asked and received, but the elder son never asked and didn't receive; and yet, no-thing was withheld from him, nor did the father expect him to work to gain it. The elder son believed he needed to perform to please his father in order to receive. We should be trusting and faithful children who ask for our inheritance knowing that the Father delights in giving to His children.

The Kingdom is the home of every believer and we have a joint-ownership in Christ for an inheritance. Your heavenly Father is not expecting you to work to receive, for the work was done by His Son on the Cross. God's desire is for you to accept what He has prepared for you.

CHAPTER TWO

THE ADAM'S

> And so it is written, The first man Adam was made a living soul; the last Adam was made a quickening spirit.
> 1 Corinthians 15:45

There is no longer a physical temple or tabernacle required for man to approach God. The veil that kept God and man separated has been ripped in two at the very moment of Christ's death on the Cross. In Christ, there is nothing preventing an intimate relationship between God and man. *And, behold, the veil of the temple was rent in twain from the top to the bottom; and the earth did quake, and the rocks rent.* Matthew 27:51 Sin was the veil, for sin cannot be where holiness reigns. The Garden of Eden was a holy paradise until sin.

There is no priest required or the blood of a sacrificial animal for the remission of our sins, for all sin and curses have been destroyed by the blood of the Lamb of God. Christ presents us to God untainted. Born of Christ's

Spirit, whether Jew or Gentile, we all are children of the Father. *There is neither Jew nor Greek, there is neither bond nor free, there is neither male nor female: for <u>ye are all one in Christ Jesus</u>.* Galatians 3:28 Also, *For there is no difference between the Jew and the Greek: for the same Lord over all is rich unto all that call upon him.* Romans 10:12

As the Word manifested the plans of God, it is the Word that His Kingdom functions on, for the Word is God. *In the beginning was the Word, and the Word was with God, and the <u>Word was God</u>.* John 1:1 Precepts or laws for both Heaven and Earth were established during the Creation; nothing to be changed. There are laws that govern the spirit Kingdom and laws that govern the earthen Kingdom.

The Word came to Earth born of flesh, and the Word hung on the Cross as the Son of Man. *And the Word was made flesh, and dwelt among us (and we behold his glory, the glory as of the only begotten of the Father,) full of grace and truth.* John 1:14 The Word came to reconcile man to the Kingdom of Heaven. We know the Word is Jesus, Son of Man, and the Word returns to the Kingdom as both Son of God and Son of Man, Christ.

There are two Adam's in God's plan. There is Adam in the Garden and Adam on the Cross; one represents the carnal man and the other the spirit of man. There are two mediators of the Word of God, Moses and Jesus. Moses for the carnal man and Christ for the spirit man. Adam brought sin in the Garden of Eden, and Christ took sin upon Himself on the Cross. Moses brought the law written on a tablet of stone for the unbelievers, while Christ brought the Spirit law written in the heart of man for all who believe. *Knowing this, that the law is not made for a righteous man, but for the lawless and disobedient, for the ungodly and for sinners, for unholy and profane, for murderers of fathers and murderers of mothers, for manslayers, For whoremongers, for them that defile themselves with mankind, for menstealers, for liars, for perjured persons, and if there be any other thing that is contrary to sound doctrine; According to the glorious gospel of the blessed God, which was committed to my trust.* 1 Timothy 1:9-11 There are carnal laws and spirit laws; therefore, be cognitive of which law you follow, for the outcome is not the same.

Before Moses became the mediator of God's Word to the Israelites, God communicated with Adam, Noah, and Abraham, the three prior covenants He had with man. This is before the law of Commandments was in effect. The Commandments were established at Creation; however, the time of Moses had not come for the carnal law to be applicable.

Adam disobeyed God when he ate from the Tree of Knowledge. He and Eve were spirit persons who lived in a perfect paradise; therefore, there was no carnal law for Him to break, but he did sin. Because of their dis-obedience, they transitioned from spirit persons to carnal, aware of their physical selves. This brought sin into the Garden of Eden and the sin nature upon man.
Though they disobeyed, they didn't break a law.

Even when their son, Cain, killed his brother Abel, the first murder recorded, there was no carnal law to judge him guilty and put to death. In fact, God placed a mark on Cain that no man could take his life. The carnal law judges; break one is to be guilty of all and the outcome is death.

Noah was the second man God established a special

covenant with prior to Abraham. These men were not sinless; however, they were not under a carnal law of Commandments. They disobeyed God's Word, but God accepted their faith and found favor in them for their belief and called them righteous in His sight. God did not judge them with a law for their sins. *But Noah found <u>grace in the eyes of the Lord</u>. These are the generations of Noah: Noah was a just man and perfect in his generations, and Noah walked with God.* Genesis 6:8-9 Also, *By faith Noah, being warned of God of things not seen as yet, moved with fear, prepared an ark to the saving of his house; by the which he condemned the world, and became <u>heir of the righteousness</u> which is by faith.* Hebrews 11:7

Abraham lied about his wife, Sarah, to Abimelech. There was no law to judge Abraham's lie. If so, he would have been found guilty and stoned to death. *And Abraham said of Sarah his wife, She is my sister: and Abimelech king of Gerar sent, and took Sarah.* Genesis 20:2 God approached Abimelech and not Abraham though it was Abraham who sinned. Abraham believed and had faith in God. *And he believed in the Lord; and he counted it to him for <u>righteousness</u>.* Genesis 15:6 And, *For what saith the scripture? Abraham believed God, and it was counted unto him for <u>righteousness</u>.* Romans 4:3 Also, *Even as Abraham believed God, and it was accounted to him for <u>righteousness</u>.* Galatians 3:6 God called Abraham a friend.

Moses, the fourth person God established a covenant with was four-hundred and thirty years after Abraham, and the first mediator of God's Word administering the Ten Commandments, a carnal law for sinful, unbelieving man. The carnal law was to show man his sin nature and that righteousness can never come through the law. *I do not frustrate the grace of God: for if righteousness come by the law, then Christ is dead in vain.* Galatians 2:21

This law was for the Jews, God's chosen people though all generations are sinners through the seed of Adam. *For <u>all have sinned</u>, and come short of the glory of God; Being justified freely by his grace through the redemption that is in Christ Jesus: Whom <u>God hath set forth to be a propitiation through faith in his blood</u>, to declare his righteousness for the remission of sins that are past, through the forbearance of God; To declare, I say, at this time his righteousness: that he might be just, and the justifier of him which believeth in Jesus.* Romans 3:23-26

The second Adam and mediator of God's Word is Christ who took man's sin and gives him righteousness as God gave to Abraham. He came to bring a new covenant for those who believe in Him. *Even the righteousness of God which is by faith of Jesus Christ unto all and upon all them that believe: for there is no difference.* Romans 3:22

The Spirit law is written in the heart of man which brings man back to the Garden of Eden before Adam sinned. *But the fruit of the Spirit is love, joy, peace, longsuffering, gentleness, goodness, faith, meekness, temperance: against such there is no law.* Galatians 5:22-23 A spirit-born person lives by spiritual laws, for they are in your heart.

The Commandments, statutes, and judgments were given to the Israelites, the Jewish populous when God removed them from slavery to King Pharaoh in Egypt. God spoke to them at Mount Sinai. The people who gathered at the base of the mountain were Jews, not

Gentiles, for the law was not given to the Gentiles. As Gentiles, we have the sin nature of Adam; however, we were not the chosen people of God.

Therefore, the law was not applicable to the Gentiles. *For as many as have sinned without law shall also perish without law: and as many as have sinned in the law shall be judged by the law; (For not the hearers of the law are just before God, but the doers of the law shall be justified.* <u>*For when the Gentiles, which have not the law,*</u> *do by nature the things contained in the law,* <u>*these, having not the law, are a law unto themselves*</u>*: Which shew the work of the law written in their hearts, their conscience also bearing witness, and their thoughts the mean while accusing or else excusing one another;) In the day when God shall judge the secrets of men by Jesus Christ according to my gospel. Romans 2:12-16*

God put a time for man's existence, seven-thousand years which correlates with His seven days of Creation, seven covenants, seven feasts, and so forth. The final one-thousand years is with Christ as our King in the Kingdom of Peace (Millennium), the seventh and final covenant with man.

The carnal law existed for a period of approximately fifteen-hundred years from Moses to Christ. There are denominations that teach the obedience of the Commandments even though they were only given to the Israelites during a specific time. The generations before Moses and after Christ weren't under the Commandments.

To be a believer whose faith is in the carnal law of the mediator Moses, a servant, rather than the mediator, Christ, the Son, negates what He did on the Cross for you. A person born of the Spirit of Christ abides by spirit laws, for they are written on your heart. *This is the covenant that I will make with them after those days, saith the Lord, <u>I will put my laws into their hearts, and in their minds will I write them</u>; And their sins and iniquities will I remember no more.* Hebrews 10:16-17 With the Holy Spirit in your heart, you live by the *Fruit of the Spirit*.

To follow Moses' carnal law when you are born of Christ's Spirit will hold you in bondage to the sin nature of Adam and gain you nothing in the Kingdom. *But now we are <u>delivered from the law</u>, that being dead wherein we were held; that we should <u>serve in newness of spirit</u>, and not in the oldness of the letter. Romans 7:6* Obedience to a law other than the spirit law given to the person born of the Spirit of God's Son is not accepting God's new covenant which came by His Son's death on the Cross. The finality of the law is death, whereby in Christ is eternal life.

When a Gentile accepts Christ as His Lord and Savior, he is adopted into the Kingdom. *Having <u>predestinated us unto the adoption of children by Jesus Christ to himself</u>, according to the good pleasure of his will, To the praise of the glory of his grace, wherein he hath made us accepted in the beloved.* Ephesians 1:5-6 There is no difference to God once born of His Son's Spirit, for God sees you righteous, absolved of the sin nature.

The Methodology of God's Plan

God designed man as a spirit person and housed the spirit in a body. He gave man a free will just as the angels in the Kingdom of Heaven. Otherwise, how would it be possible for Lucifer and one-third of the angels to go against their Almighty King? *So God created man in his own image, in the image of God created he him; male and female created he them.* Genesis 1:27 It is by their free will, soulful thought, that Adam and Eve disobeyed God, just as it is by our free will to accept Him.

How we use our free will determines the direction our life takes just as it did for Adam and Eve in the Garden. In not acknowledging the second Adam, we remain under the first Adam. What does this mean? We receive a sin nature through the disobedience of the first Adam, while the second Adam redeems man from everything the first Adam caused.

Even after accepting Christ, it is possible to remain under the first Adam's nature of being sin-conscious by continuing to follow an old covenant. The old covenant of Moses is for the carnal, sinful man to remind him of his sins and that he needs a savior. When you don't see yourself forgiven in Christ, but continue to hold shame, guilt, condemnation, and feelings of unworthiness, you are held captive in the old covenant.

Christ has given you a new covenant made on better promises. *But now hath he obtained a more excellent ministry, by how much also he is the mediator of a better covenant, which was established upon better promises.* Hebrews 8:6 Depending upon which Adam and covenant you believe will affect your life, present and future tense. When you choose to be born into the Kingdom of Heaven, it is a conscious decision to want a covenant in Christ. Whether Jew or Gentile, you are of the body of Christ and governed by the spirit laws of the Kingdom.

Your spirit is now awakened. You have a body and soul but also are a spirit person; however, it should no longer be the soul (self-righteous) in charge of the body, but rather the spirit (righteous) in command of the soul and body. *Therefore if any man be in Christ, he is <u>a new creature</u>: old things are passed away; behold, all things are become new.* 2 Corinthians 5:17 The old sinful man has died on the Cross in Christ and the new spirit person is born. *Now if <u>we be dead with Christ</u>, we believe that we shall also <u>live with him</u>.* Romans 6:8

Born in the Spirit, you are *in* the world but not *of* the world. *I pray not that thou shouldest take them out of the world, but that thou shouldest keep them from the evil. They are not of the world, even as I am not of the world.* John 17:15-16 As a believer, you remain in this earthen world physically, but you are spirit-born for the Kingdom of God.

You look in the mirror and see the same reflection, and perhaps feel no different, but your life has changed forever. *But if the Spirit of him that raised up Jesus from the dead <u>dwell in you</u>, he that raised up Christ from the dead shall also <u>quicken your mortal bodies by his Spirit that dwelleth in you</u>.* Romans 8:11 Once your spirit is awakened, God is in you. *Know ye not that ye are the temple of God, and that <u>the Spirit of God dwelleth in you</u>?* 1 Corinthians 3:16 This is a powerful realization, for you have God with you.

As Christ is in the Kingdom, so are you with Him because He is in you and you are in Him. Where you are so is He, and where He is so are you. This is important to grasp, for it is the beginning of your spirit life. Know your position in Christ. *But God, who is rich in mercy, for his great love wherewith he loved us, Even when we were dead in sins, hath quickened us together with Christ, (by grace ye are saved;) And hath raised us up together, and made us sit together in heavenly places in Christ Jesus: That in the ages to come he might shew the exceeding riches of his grace in his kindness toward us through Christ Jesus.* Ephesians 2:4-7

We renew our mind to the principles that govern the Spirit Kingdom, for these are the laws for our new spirit life. *And be not conformed to this world: but be ye transformed by the renewing of your mind, that ye may prove what is that good, and acceptable, and perfect, will of God.* Romans 12:2 Not only do we change the way we think, but change who we depend on, for we seek wisdom from the *Spirit of Truth*. Our focus is always on the Father and the Son.

Born of Christ's Spirit, we live as His bride until He returns to resurrect us with a new body (without blood) and takes us to our new home. Until then, we remain on Earth living according to the spirit Kingdom, not the earthen one. Our reliance is on God, not man.

As in most conventional marriages, there typically is joint-ownership of properties and this holds true in our relationship with Christ. *And if children, then heirs; heirs of God, and joint-heirs with Christ.* Romans 8:17 It's like bringing a person you want to marry to your parents for their approval. You have already made the decision to marry this individual, but you'd like their blessings. Same is true of accepting Christ; you agreed to a relationship with Him, a covenant. Christ brings you before the Father sanctified to take residency within the Kingdom.

Our position in Christ is relevant to receiving spiritual gifts. In Christ, we have the Spirit of God. *I and my Father are one.* John 10:30 As Jesus told His disciples: *If ye had known me, ye should have known my Father also: and from henceforth ye know him, and have seen him.* John 14:7 We sometimes falter in realizing that it is God in us and with us at all times as He is Christ and the Holy Spirit.

God has given all things both in Heaven and on Earth to His Son and because we have an inheritance in Christ, we are given entitlement to all the treasures within the Kingdom. *The Father loveth the Son, and hath <u>given all things into his hand</u>.* John 3:35 As the Father gives to His Son, the Son gives to the children of the Father. *And I will <u>give unto you the keys of the kingdom of heaven</u>: and <u>whatsoever thou shalt bind on earth shall be bound in heaven</u>: and whatsoever thou shalt loose on earth shall be loosed in heaven.* Matthew 16:19

Your life depends on the finished work of God's Son on the Cross. Making the transition from carnal to spirit person places you, spiritually, into the Kingdom until the day comes and you live eternally in your new home.

Below is a comparison of the two Adam's and what each brings to man beginning in the Garden of Eden and ending in the Garden of Gethsemane, before Christ is crucified. Christ's death on the Cross brought all things to fruition.

1st Adam	**2nd Adam**
Garden of Eden	Garden of Gethsemane
Seed/Carnal Man	Spirit/Spirit Person
Sin	Saint
Carnal Law	Spirit Law
Mediator/Moses	Mediator/Christ
Old Covenant	New Covenant
Judged	Redeemed
Death	Eternal Life

CHAPTER THREE

THE SON

*Whosoever shall confess that Jesus is the
Son of God, God dwelleth in him,
and he in God.*
1 John 4:15

It is important to acknowledge the two distinctive roles of Christ. He is the Son of God; and yet, He became the Son of Man when born of flesh. Understanding Christ as Son of Man on Earth and Son of God in the Kingdom will strengthen your relationship with Him.

We know it is the *Word who* came to Earth. The *Word* is the *Son of God* and *Son of Man;* He is all God and all man. God from the Spirit Kingdom and man for the earthen Kingdom. *Whosoever shall confess that Jesus is the <u>Son of God</u>, God dwelleth in him, and he in God.* 1

John 4:15 Also, *The beginning of the gospel of Jesus Christ, the <u>Son of God</u>.* Mark 1:1 And, *But that ye may know that the <u>Son of man</u> hath power on earth to forgive sins.* Matthew 9:6 Also, *For the <u>Son of man</u> is Lord even of the sabbath day.* Matthew 12:8 There are numerous Scriptures depicting Christ as Son of God and Son of Man.

While on Earth, the Son did not use His deity as Son of God, but only lived as a physical person, Son of Man. Christ knew His role as Son of Man and what He would need to do for man's sake. Even at an early age of twelve when He sat in the synagogue with the elders, they were amazed at His intellect. When Joseph and Mary came for Him having thought Him lost, what did Jesus say to His parents: *And he said unto them, How is it that ye sought me? wist ye not that <u>I must be about my Father's business</u>? And they understood not the saying which he spake unto them.* Luke 2:49-50

He often explained to His disciples His purpose on Earth. *For I came down from heaven, not to do mine own will, but the will of him that sent me.* John 6:38 And, *Jesus saith unto them, My meat is to do the will of him that sent me, and to finish his work.* John 4:34 Also, *But Jesus answered them, My Father worketh hitherto, and I work.* John 5:17

He came to teach of another world and of a Father, a King, who loves us. Christ served the people as Son of Man and continues today from the throne as Son of God.

Before there was Adam, there was no personage of the Father and the Son. There was God and the Word manifesting the Creation and then on the sixth day, man was created for the Kingdom of Earth and placed in the Garden of Eden. Adam was in charge of the Kingdom of

Earth until Lucifer stole his Kingdom through deceit.

Though the second Adam was before the first Adam, it wasn't until the fall of the first Adam that the second Adam became the Son of Man. *And so it is written, The first man Adam was made a living soul; the last Adam was made a quickening spirit.* 1 Corinthians 15:45 It was already planned by God at His Divine Creation what would be required to save man from death.

The Almighty King came down from His throne to live among the people to take back what was stolen in the Garden. Christ taught of a Kingdom that was not of this world. *And he said unto them, Ye are from beneath; I am from above: ye are of this world; <u>I am not of this world</u>.* John 8:23 Also, Jesus stated: *<u>My kingdom is not of this world</u>: if my kingdom were of this world, then would my servants fight, that I should not be delivered to the Jews: but now is my kingdom not from hence.* John 18:36

When the prophesied time comes, it will be the Son of God who destroys Lucifer, but it was the Son of Man who died on the Cross for man. Sin had to be dealt with in the flesh, just as Lucifer will be dealt with in the spirit, for He is a fallen archangel, a spirit being. There is a timeline and order to God's Kingdom.

While Christ was on Earth He had many titles, more than fifty recorded in the Scriptures. Though they are all significant, perhaps the most acknowledged are the *Word*, the *Living Water*, the *Bread of Life*, *the Light of the World*, the *Prince of Peace*, the *Lamb of God*, and the *Good Shepherd*, for each tells of what He gives to man. He is our Shepherd, we are His flock, and He came to gather us unto Himself.

The King came to Earth and served the people. *Even as the <u>Son of man</u> came not to be ministered unto, <u>but to</u>*

minister, and to give his life a ransom for many. Matthew 20:28 God came not only to teach but humbled Himself to serve. When He healed, raised the dead, and washed the feet of His disciples, He was serving the people. He taught, He served, and He sacrificed Himself for man.

We've been taught such a watered-down version of Christ that we completely miss the magnitude of His mission. He served as a man and when He returned to His throne, He serves as our Lord. There is much to what Christ has done so man can have a place in the Kingdom of Heaven.

In most denominations, we accept Christ as the Son of God who died on the Cross for our sins and gives us salvation, but the ministerial teachings stop short. Some will mention that we receive the gift of the Holy Spirit when we repent and accept Jesus as our Lord and Savior, but there is no explanation of His role in our life.

The magnificence of what the Son has done because of the Father's love should be humbling. God's desire is for you to be born of His Son's Spirit and be with Him in His Kingdom. Your Almighty King came to this corrupt world to seek you; however, He will not coerce you into a relationship, for He will not go against the free will He gave to you. It remains your choice.

When the Father gave ownership of Heaven and Earth to His Son, the Son then gives you the authority of His name. *Jesus knowing that the Father had given all things into his hands, and that he was come from God, and went to God.* John 13:3 You have a position of authority in Christ within the Kingdom, unlike the angels. In your relationship in Christ to live by the Word of God, you have access to supernatural heavenly power.

Remaining unaware of these truths makes it possible

for your inheritance to be stolen by the thief who comes to steal, kill, and destroy anything that God has for you. Lucifer wants to destroy not just your relationship with God and His Son, but set chaos, disharmony, and destruction in your life and family.

This is a spiritual battle and Satan runs interference and literally blocks you from knowing the truth of your Almighty King, accepting your rightful position in Christ, and receiving the promises of the Father. Satan's best strategy is keeping you ignorant to the Kingdom principles, for this is the knowledge, wisdom, and power of God.

God's Kingdom functions on His Word. It was the *Word of God* at the foundation, the *Word* taught on Earth, His *Word* given to the disciples to carry the gospel, it is on the authority of His *Word* that we pray, and it remains His *Word* that we are to live by and proclaim. This is the essence of what Lucifer doesn't want you to learn, for power is in the Word of God.

In the Old Testament, God removed the people from slavery and told them He was their God who loved them and would provide and care for them, give them a homeland of fertile land, cattle, and vineyards; and yet, they refused by default of worshipping other gods. They didn't believe in Him, nor want Him to be their King. In fact, they were afraid of God and asked Moses to be their spokesperson, but God had already planned for Moses to be the mediator making a covenant with the people.

It wasn't until after forty years and the generation died off because of their unbelief that their children, who believed God, were given the land to inhabit, the one promised to their forefathers. After Moses' death,

Joshua led them to the land God had promised. For four-thousand years until Christ, God dealt with the people.

Christ spent His time teaching of a King who wanted to be a Father to the people. Miracles revealed to them He was who He said He was and came from a Kingdom they had yet to know and that an eternal life awaited those who believed in Him.

He anointed His disciples to continue His ministry. They were given supernatural power through the Holy Spirit to continue performing miracles, healing, and raise the dead. *And when he had so said, he shewed unto them his hands and his side. Then were the disciples glad, when they saw the Lord. Then said Jesus to them again, Peace be unto you: as my Father hath sent me, even so send I you. And when he had said this, he breathed on them, and saith unto them, Receive ye the Holy Ghost.* John 20:20-22 Today, He gives you the same Holy Spirit.

There are many who teach *of* God but not *about* Him. They speak *of* Christ, but not *about* His role, His work, and His truth. How can you have a relationship with Christ, if you don't know the person? How can you expect to receive from God if you don't understand the methodology for the manifestation? It is something to consider.

Know the sacrifice of the Son of Man and what the Son of God gives to you as He sits on His throne. Whether on the Cross or in the Kingdom, Christ is serving you because of the love the Father has for you.

CHAPTER FOUR

RIGHTEOUSNESS

But of him are ye in Christ Jesus, who of God is made unto us wisdom, and righteousness, and sanctification, and redemption: That, according as it is written, He that glorieth, let him glory in the Lord.
1 Corinthians 1:30-31

To have a relationship with Christ requires more than believing. It is accepting a marriage covenant, for you are His bride. *Wherefore, my brethren, ye also are become dead to the law by the body of Christ; that ye should be <u>married to another, even to him who is raised from the dead</u>, that we should bring forth fruit unto God.* Romans 1:4 Eve was made from Adam's rib, a physical body; and in Christ, we are birthed from a physical body to a spirit person. Eve was Adam's bride, we are Christ's bride.

Many are unaware they have a marriage covenant with Christ. Most teachings concentrate on the forgiveness of sins and salvation missing altogether the significance of the relationship. Just as we learn the nature of a person we may consider in marriage, so should we know Christ's finished work, for it establishes our position with Him within the Kingdom. As His bride, we have privileges to the treasures which are meant for our earthen life. To receive, we have to know how to release the blessings.

Born of the Spirit of Christ, your position is one of righteousness. You have been sanctified by His blood for the Kingdom. *And be found in him, not having mine own righteousness, which is of the law, but that which is through the faith of Christ, <u>the righteousness which is of God by faith</u>.* Philippians 3:9 Also, *Even the righteousness of God which is by faith of Jesus Christ unto all and upon all them that believe: for there is no difference.* Romans 3:22

As a bride, you have privileges to use the authority of Christ's name and call upon that which is not seen to be. If you need better relations with family and friends, a healing, a miracle, released from addiction, prosperity such as employment, and so forth, you may call on the Word of God. *And whatsoever <u>ye shall ask in my name, that will I do</u>, that the Father may be glorified in the Son.* John 14:13 Your position in Christ enables you to receive that which you need.

For example in your family, you may ask to borrow an item and typically because of the love in the relationship it is supplied. It is no different within the Kingdom.

God is rich with gifts to give you because He loves you.

Acknowledging your righteous position is to make the transition from sinner to saint. Change the way you think and renew your mind to the new person you are in Christ. *And be not conformed to this world: but be <u>ye transformed by the renewing of your mind</u>, that ye may prove what is that good, and acceptable, and perfect, will of God.* Romans 12:2 This is the beginning of living in the spirit Kingdom.

Be mindful of your relationship in Christ and know that He is always with you. *<u>Abide in me, and I in you</u>. As the branch cannot bear fruit of itself, except it abide in the vine; no more can ye, except ye abide in me.* John 15:4 Christ enables you to have a relationship with the Father. *For the Lord God is a sun and shield: the Lord will give grace and glory: <u>no good thing will he withhold from them that walk uprightly</u>.* Psalm 84:11

We depend on the covenant Christ has given. If we only accept His death on the Cross for forgiveness of sins, but aren't living by the Word of God, we negate what He did. Our sins are removed and we have salvation; however, we can restrict the promises of God. *I do not <u>frustrate the grace of God</u>: for if righteousness come by the law, then Christ is dead in vain.* Galatians 2:21 Many believers continue to live as though nothing has changed when everything changes for the person born in Christ.

A person can believe in Christ and not be living with the new covenant. *And for this cause <u>he is the mediator of the new testament</u>, that by means of death, for the redemption of the transgressions that were under the first testament, they which are called might receive the promise of eternal inheritance.* Hebrews 9:15 Also, *But now* *hath he obtained a more excellent ministry, by how much also he is <u>the mediator of a better covenant</u>, which was established upon better promises.* Hebrews 8:6 And, *But this shall be the covenant that I will make with the house of Israel; After those days, saith the Lord, I will put my law in their inward parts, and <u>write it in their hearts</u>; and will be their God, and they shall be my people.* Jeremiah 31:33 The new covenant is the foundation for a righteous life.

Unfortunately, many do not seek their inheritance, but rely on man's wisdom rather than the authority they have as a bride to Christ. *That your faith should not stand in the wisdom of men, but in the power of God.* 1 Corinthians 2:5 It requires being dependent on supernatural power through the Holy Spirit rather than the elements of the world.

Grace is the foundation whereby God's Kingdom principles are founded. The blessings flow through grace, and Christ gives us grace and truth. *For the law was given by Moses, but grace and truth came by Jesus Christ.* John 1:17 Though grace is always present, it is our faith that releases grace into our life. Know your position in Christ within the Kingdom, so that you may receive all that the Father and the Son have for you. *If <u>ye abide in me, and my words abide in you</u>, ye shall ask what ye will, and <u>it shall be done unto you</u>.* John 15:7

Recall Abraham lived four-hundred and thirty years before Moses administered the law to the Jews and because Abraham believed in God's Word, God accounted righteousness unto him. *For the promise, that he should be the heir of the world, was not to Abraham, or to his seed, through the law, but through the <u>righteousness of</u>*

faith. Romans 4:13 Abraham was faithful to God. Our faith exemplifies our righteousness in the Son of God.

Everyone will stand before Christ. *For we must all appear before the judgment seat of Christ; that every one may receive the things done in his body, according to that he hath done, whether it be good or bad.* 2 Corinthians 5:10 Wouldn't you want to stand as a bride who lived faithful to God's Word by abiding in His Son?

Everyday proclaim your position in Christ for the Father. Say out loud:

I am the righteousness in Christ, the bride of the Son of God. I live by the Word of God, and am grounded in His grace and truth with the presence and power of the Holy Spirit. My faith is in my Most High God, Amen.

Believe it and hold it firm in your heart. Know that you belong to God because of the finished work of His Son on the Cross.

CHAPTER FIVE

REST

Let us therefore fear, lest, a promise being left us of entering into his rest, any of you should seem to come short of it. For unto us was the gospel preached, as well as unto them: but the word preached did not profit them, not being mixed with faith in them that heard it. For we which have believed do enter into rest, as he said, As I have sworn in my wrath, if they shall enter into my rest: although the works were finished from the foundation of the world. For he spake in a certain place of the seventh day on this wise, And God did rest the seventh day from all his works.
Hebrews 4:1-4

God rested on the seventh day of His Creation as all His work was finished, nothing to ever be changed. Christ announced the Father's work was finished on the Cross, nothing more to be done. What does *although the works were finished from the foundation of the world* mean to you? It defines from Creation to Cross everything has been accomplished and set forth for your life.

God planned a life for Adam and Eve, a life for the Israelites, and has prepared a life for you. At the time of His Creation, every person was given a plan, for God provides for all the people even those who don't believe. For example, He rained manna from Heaven to the Israelites in the wilderness while in their unbelief. However, the difference for those who receive and those who don't is resting in His truth. We are to rest in the knowledge of His promises and trust in His Word, for all the blessings come from this foundation.

Adam and Eve rested in God's Word until deception changed their thinking. The generation led by Joshua into the land God promised to their forefathers rested in the Word of God. They changed their thinking from their father's belief to one of trusting God. When we change our thoughts to be focused on what God has already made available rather than on what can we get Him to do, we rest in the knowledge of receiving His blessings, for this is His plan for you.

Your efforts will never get God to move in your life. Give the problem to God and rest with faith and patience that He already has a provision knowing the very day this matter would require His intervention, but you must allow His presence.

We all want what our heavenly Father has to give, but we don't know how to get it. We simply lack in the wisdom to bring down what is in Heaven to this earthen world. It isn't diligent praying to get God to do something, but know that He planned what you will need. Our prayer is one of thanking our heavenly Father for what He has done, not pleading with Him. If you want His provisions of healing, a miracle, and prosperity for better relations, released from addictions, a job promotion, and more, it's received through trusting it has been taken care of, not will God do it. We need to change the way we think about God, and how He provides His blessings.

This can be a difficult realization for some to grasp. It's our human nature to want to get involved and put our own efforts into resolving a matter; therefore, to rely on someone else, God, goes against our instincts. However, if we don't do exactly that, we are sabotaging God's plan with our efforts.

Trying to solve a problem by our own merit and then ask for God's intervention is blocking the Holy Spirit's supernatural power. However, when we give it to God and trust Him to handle the matter, He will resolve the issue because we trusted Him for it. *Let us therefore fear, lest, a promise being left us of <u>entering into his rest</u>, any of you should seem to come short of it. Hebrews 4:1*

There is no confusion, frustration, or worry when we rest in God. Instead, there is peace and calmness in a crisis. *Come unto me, all ye that labour and are heavy laden, and <u>I will give you rest</u>. Take my yoke upon you, and <u>learn of me</u>; for I am meek and lowly in heart: and ye shall <u>find rest unto your souls</u>.* Matthew 11:28-30 God expects us to rest, for it is the only way His promises can be released in our life.

If our faith is based on the idea that we must work to please God, or want to place our own thoughts, ideas, or performance into a situation, we obstruct God. We are using our natural abilities and preventing the super-natural power from manifesting. *Now to him that worketh is the reward not reckoned of grace, but of debt. But to him that <u>worketh not, but believeth on him that justifieth the ungodly,</u> <u>his faith is counted for righteousness</u>.* Romans 4:4-5 It cannot be a combination of our efforts and God's power. There aren't two drivers behind the wheel of a vehicle at the same time. Either we are in control or God, but never both simultaneously.

For example, if you take a credit card and cut it in half holding one half of the card, it has no buying power; however, should you take the whole card to the store you can make purchases. If you only believe in God's Word, but aren't applying His principles in your life, you are restricting His power. It is not enough to believe; after all, Satan believes.

God's provisions begin the day you accept His Son's Spirit. Christ gives you the Holy Spirit who releases what you need into your life. With maturing in God's Word, we learn the principles of His Kingdom to understand how to release what He has appropriated.

The Holy Spirit gives us the knowledge and wisdom to live by the Word of God. His nine gifts are for the sole purpose of providing for our needs from giving us knowledge of God's Word to performing miracles. *For to one is given by the Spirit the word of **wisdom**; to another the word of **knowledge** by the same Spirit; To another **faith** by the same Spirit; to another the gifts of **healing** by the same Spirit; To another the working of **miracles**; to another **prophecy**; to another **discerning of spirits;** to another **divers kinds of tongues**; to another the **interpretation of tongues**: But all these worketh that one and the selfsame Spirit, dividing to every man severally as he* *will.* 1 Corinthians 12:8-11 There is no situation that God hasn't covered in these gifts.

It is realizing the work has been done and your part is to receive. Rest in the knowledge that the Father and His Son have prepared *provisions* for your every need from the moment you are born into this physical world to the moment you leave it, and beyond. When you rest, God works; however, when you work with your efforts, God steps back. God will not get in the way of your free will, for it would be going against the very gift He gave to man. You can use your free will to be dependent upon yourself, or trust in your heavenly Father.

Unfortunately, what typically occurs when a person accepts Christ is they continue life unaware they have authority and supernatural power given to them. This explains why so many aren't receiving answers to prayers. God has your solutions ready for you like a package waiting to be claimed, but lack of understanding His Kingdom principles inhibits you from picking up your goods. *Beloved, I wish above all things that thou mayest prosper and be in health, even as they soul prospereth. 3 John 1:2* It isn't God's fault if you don't claim His gifts.

To not accept what has been given by God and fulfilled by His Son can be construed as a rejection by omission of His plan for you. They aren't withholding; however, because of not accepting what they have done prohibits their plan being effectual in your life.

Know the principles God established that govern your ability to live within His Kingdom, spiritually, and receive the storehouse of treasures He has set forth for you. Everything required for a healthy, productive, and successful life is available to receive at anytime. The key is to rest in your righteous position in Christ because you trust in your Lord. *Rest* in the Word of God, *rest* in the finished work of the Son, *rest* in the knowledge that God's favor is upon you, and *rest* in knowing that God already has the provisions you need for any circumstance.

The Son's finished work reveals God's plan for you.

CHAPTER SIX

THE CHOICE

*I have no greater joy than to
hear that my children walk in truth.*
3 John 1:4

God wants everyone to live in His Kingdom where a place has been prepared for you. Jesus explained to His disciples: *In my Father's house are many mansions: if it were not so, I would have told you. I go to prepare a place for you.* John 14:2 Christ is that preparation. When He said, *I go to prepare a place for you,* Jesus is referring to Himself knowing what is required at the Cross. He became our passage into the Kingdom when He took our punishment. God has *many mansions* in anticipation of His children.

For the believer, it requires living by the Word of God

taught by the Spirit of Truth. *In the beginning was the Word, and the Word was with God, and <u>the Word was God</u>.* John 1:1 It is God as the Son of Man born of flesh to live on Earth and who took our place on the Cross, God as the Son who births us in His Spirit, and God as the Holy Spirit who dwells in the heart of man. The three personages of God. *Know ye not that ye are the temple of God, and that the <u>Spirit of God dwelleth in you</u>?* 1 Corinthians 3:16 God created you for Himself; however, do you truly live for your heavenly Father?

God provides through His grace and we receive by our faith. Grace is always present supplying the blessings of the Father, and it is our faith that secures His gifts in our life. We receive because we accept, we accept because we believe, we believe because we have faith, and we have faith because we trust the finished work of Christ on the Cross.

It must be a true faith in God and His Kingdom and not a misguided faith that is tainted with unbelief. If we trust in a doctrine that is not grounded in the work of the Father and the Son, and not allow ourselves to be taught by the tutor God has given, then our diluted faith restricts receiving heavenly treasures.

There is an undeniable plan of our Almighty King. His work from Creation to the Cross has been *about* you and *for* you. He has loved you before you were conceived for a birth into this earthen world because He has known you as the spirit person He created for His Kingdom. His deepest desire is that you accept His invitation to His home. The invite has been delivered by His Son.

Though we acknowledge the Trinity of God in the personages of Father, Son, and Holy Spirit, it is wise to know our Creator as an Almighty King, a Most High God.

It is because of His everlasting, unadulterated, unfiltered, never-changing and unconditional love that He gives you an eternal life with Him, for He has always loved you.

God gives a continuous flow of blessings to the children who are faithful to His Word, trust in His Son, and depend on the Holy Spirit. This is the profound truth of living spirit-born within the Kingdom of Heaven today and forever. The question to consider is what kingdom are you dependent upon, earthen or spirit, for they never can be combined.

Many are ill-equipped in the knowledge of God's Kingdom precepts by holding onto false doctrines believing them to be truth. Christians, in general, are too quick to accept the world rather than the Kingdom. God is His *Kingdom*, His *Word*, and His *Power* which means you have everything of God within you.

What does this mean, exactly? It means that God as the Holy Spirit and as Christ is giving you *authority* and *power*. It requires speaking out loud that which you need. *For verily I say unto you, That whosoever shall <u>say</u> unto this mountain, Be thou removed, and be thou cast into the sea; and shall not doubt in his heart, but shall believe that those things which he <u>saith</u> shall come to pass; he shall have whatsoever he <u>saith</u>.* Mark 11:23 Jesus stated three times to speak out loud.

Just as God spoke His Creation into existence, and Christ's declaration was spoken out loud on the Cross, so must we speak out loud on the authority of Christ. The mountain is the problem and when you voice your command, you are expressing your faith on the authority in Christ with the power of the Holy Spirit to see results. You proclaim the everlasting Word of God by speaking out loud.

Christ also tells us: *And whatsoever ye shall ask in my name, that will I do, that the Father may be glorified in the Son.* John 14:13 When you trust in God with praise and thanksgiving letting your request be known, you will have the manifestation, for God has your resolution from the end to the beginning of your life. Glorify Him with praise for what He has done for you.

Christ sent the Holy Spirit to His disciples and instructed them they had the power to heal, perform miracles, and raise the dead as they continued His ministry. He gives you the same supernatural power for your earthen circumstances. As Jesus required the Spirit of God, the disciples received the Spirit of God, so does our life require the Spirit of God. The Holy Spirit, the power of God, is within you.

When a crisis occurs, are you seeing the situation strictly with carnal eyes, or are you applying spiritual discernment? Do you make it your reality, or rebuke it on the authority of Christ? What you speak will be your faith; therefore, your faith determines success or failure.

God's Word is His power. *Death and life are in the power of the tongue: and they that love it shall eat the fruit thereof.* Proverbs 18:21 There is power in the words you speak for life or death, good or evil, and the fruit (results) will be determine by what you believe, what you say, and what you hold in faith to be your truth.

Knowing you have the presence of God, you can say to the situation, I do not accept this (and state what it is) rejecting it and turn it over to God. By not claiming the negative and knowing God has a provision, it only requires you holding faith. Technically and theoretically, God has to resolve the matter because you rest in His Word and wait patiently for the manifestation. The Father doesn't go against His Word, for He is the Word.

It is profound that many simply will not comprehend this knowledge of God. What you believe will render the outcome, just as what you say expresses the power of God to heal, to produce a miracle, to raise the dead, to remove addictions, to bring prosperity, or anything that is needed.

If you were given a box of wonderful items such as healing, miracles, improved marital relations, freedom from addictions, better employment, a new home, and so forth, what would you do? Would you stare at the box and never open it, or would you want access to all those magnificent gifts that will give you a good life? The answer should seem clear; however, not so. Many who see themselves faithful will not open the chest of God's blessings. Not so hard to understand if they lack wisdom of God's Kingdom. This is where the children of God can be lost to His provisions.

If you are hoping only for an eternal afterlife, you are missing all that God intended for you to have today. You have heavenly treasures at your disposal. What are you doing with your gifts?

SUMMARY

*And we have known and believed the love
that God hath to us. God is love; and he that
dwelleth in love dwelleth in God,
and God in him.*
1 John 4:16

Life is about choices and we strive to make sure our decisions produce good results. We are born with an intuitive and instinctive nature and have learned to depend on ourselves. However, to depend on God is also a learned behavior. It's about a relationship, one we don't take seriously. We are unfamiliar with Kingdom precepts, understanding Christ's finished work on the Cross, unaware of a new covenant and inheritance, and falter in the wisdom of living in the spirit realm. This is a hinderance to the promises of the Father.

Like any relationship, it's as strong as the time invested. The more you seek God's Word, the more intimate the relationship becomes. As you gain wisdom through the *Spirit of Truth*, the easier it is to witness the truth. God and His Son have finished their work and now you have a responsibility in the relationship which is to receive what they have done. We receive the favor of God through His grace by our faith.

God states He will give the keys to His Kingdom, so that what is in Heaven can be brought down to Earth. *And I will give unto thee the keys of the kingdom of heaven: and whatsoever thou shalt bind on earth shall be bound in heaven: and whatsoever thou shalt loose on earth shall be loosed in heaven.* Matthew 16:19

He is stating the provisions are available, but we need to position ourselves to receive them. Jesus said: *I am the vine, ye are the branches:* <u>*He that abideth in me, and I in him,*</u> *the same bringeth forth much fruit: for without me ye can do nothing.* John 15:5 Christ is our position within the Kingdom. Believe in the finished work of Christ on the Cross, for He sacrificed that you can be sanctified.

Grace is the foundation and the Holy Spirit is the pathway to the heavenly treasures for our earthen life. We should rely on the Holy Spirit's discerning of God's Word, so that when we hear someone speak, we will know it to be truth, or not. *Howbeit when he, the Spirit of truth, is come,* <u>*he will guide you into all truth*</u>*: for he shall not speak of himself; but whatsoever he shall hear, that shall he speak: and he will shew you things to come. He shall glorify me: for he shall receive of mine, and shall shew it unto you.* John 16:13-14 The Holy Spirit is our witness to the Word of God.

God has a plan for everyone's life. He knew you before you were born, knows the number of hairs on your head, knows everything about your life, even when you will leave this earthen place. He knows your life from the end to the beginning and has a provision for every situation you may encounter. Wouldn't you want a close relationship with someone who loves you this much?

It is imperative to understand God's principles, what the Son fulfilled at the Cross, and our position as a spirt-born person, so that we can have a relationship with the Father and the Son and receive the authority and power given to us who are born into the Kingdom.

Christ's death made all things possible, so you can go where no man can be without Him. As His bride, He gives you gifts that no man could ever fashion, and they are forever. His home is a palace designed especially for you, a Kingdom with many mansions.

God came down to Earth for you, to bring you home; a magnificent expression of the everlasting love of the Father. God is love, and God loves you!

He that loveth not knoweth not God;
for God is love.
1 John 4:8

EXCERPTS

Everlasting Love, God's Greatest Gift

EXTRACTS

Evaluating Lovewood Observations

SEVEN FINAL WORDS OF CHRIST ON THE CROSS

As Christ hung on the Cross at Golgotha, outside of Jerusalem, He spoke seven times before succumbing to His death. God's holy number, seven.

THE FIRST WORD

Then said Jesus, Father, forgive them; for they know not what they do. Luke 23:34

THE SECOND WORD

And he said to Jesus, Lord, remember me when thou comest into thy kingdom. And Jesus said unto him, Verily, I say to unto thee, to day shalt thou be with me in paradise. Luke 23:42-43

THE THIRD WORD

When Jesus therefore saw his mother, and the disciple standing by, whom he loved, he saith unto his mother, Woman, behold thy son! Then saith he to the disciple, Behold thy mother! And from that hour that disciple took her unto his home. John 19:26-27

THE FOURTH WORD

And about the ninth hour, Jesus cried with a loud voice, saying, Eli, Eli, lama sabachthani? That is to say, My God, my God, why have you forsaken me? Matthew 27:46; Mark 15:34

THE FIFTH WORD

Jesus cried out in a loud voice, Father, into your hands I commend my spirit. Luke 23:46

THE SIXTH WORD

After this, Jesus knowing that all things were now accomplished, that the scripture might be fulfilled, saith, I thirst. John 19:28

THE SEVENTH WORD

Now there was set a vessel full of vinegar: and they filled a sponge with vinegar, and put it upon hyssop, and put it to his mouth. When Jesus therefore received the vinegar, he said, It is finished: and he bowed his head, and gave up the ghost. John 19:29-30

THE TRINITY IN CHRIST

In studying the Trinity of God, we witness the relevance of God's Creation and all that was fashioned at the foundation was defined in His Son, Christ, the Word. *For by him were all things created, that are in heaven, and that are in earth, visible and invisible, whether they be thrones, or dominions, or principalities, or powers: all things were created by him, and for him: And he is before all things, and by him all things consist.* Colossians 1:16-17 We see the completion through the nature, position, and work of Christ as Son of God and Son of Man.

<u>The Nature of Christ</u>

CHIEF CORNERSTONE – Jesus is the cornerstone of the building which is His church. He cements together Jew and Gentile, male and female; all saints from all ages and places into one structure built on faith in Him which is shared by all. *And are built upon the foundation of the apostles and prophets, Jesus Christ himself being the* **chief corner stone***; In whom all the building fitly framed together groweth unto an holy temple in the Lord.* Ephesians 2:20-21

FIRSTBORN OVER ALL CREATION - Not the first thing God created, but that Christ occupies the rank and pre-eminence of the firstborn over all things, that He sustains the most exalted rank in the universe. He is preeminent above all others; He is at the head of all things. *Who is the image of the invisible God, the* **firstborn** *of every creature: For by him were all things created, that are in heaven, and that are in earth, visible and invisible, whether they be thrones, or dominions, or principalities, or powers: all things were created by him, and for him: and he is before all things, and by all things consist.* Colossians 1:15-16

HEAD OF THE CHURCH - Jesus Christ, not a king or a pope, is the only supreme, sovereign ruler of the people, the Church. *And hath put all things under his feet, and gave him to be the head over all things to the church, Which is his body, the fulness of him that filleth all in all.* Also, *For the husband is the head of the wife, even as Christ is the* **head of the church**: *and he is the saviour of the body.* Ephesians 1:22-23; 5:23

HOLY ONE - Christ is holy, both in His divine and human nature, and the fountain of holiness to His people. By His death, we are made holy and pure before God. *But ye denied the* **Holy One** *and the Just, and desired a mur-derer to be granted unto you; And killed the Prince of life, whom God hath raised from the dead; whereof we are witnesses.* Also, *For thou will not leave my soul in hell; neither wilt thou suffer thine* **Holy One** *to see corruption.* Acts 3:14; Psalm 16:10

JUDGE - The Lord Jesus was appointed by God to judge the world and to dispense the rewards of eternity.

And he commanded us to preach unto the people, and to testify that it is he which was ordained of God to be the **Judge** *of quick and dead. Also, Henceforth there is laid up for me a crown of righteousness, which the Lord, the righteous* **Judge**, *shall give me at that day: and not to me only, but unto all them also that love his appearing. And, And hath given him authority to execute judgment also, because he is the Son of man; For the Lord is our* **Judge**, *the Lord is our lawgiver, the Lord is our king; he will save us.* Acts 10:42; 2 Timothy 4:8; John 5:27

KING OF KINGS AND LORD OF LORDS – Jesus is King and has dominion over all authority on the earth, over all kings and rulers of this world. *Which in his times he shall show, who is the blessed and only Potentate, the* **King of kings, and Lord of lords**. *Also, And he hath on his vesture and on his thigh a name written,* **King of kings, and Lord of Lords**. 1 Timothy 6:15; Revelation 19:16

LIGHT OF THE WORLD – Jesus came into a world darkened by sin and shed the light of life and truth through His work and His words. *Then spake Jesus unto them, saying, I am the* **light of the world**: *he that followeth me shall not walk in darkness, but shall have the light of life.* John 8:12

PRINCE OF PEACE – Jesus came to bring peace to the world and remove the sin that came between God and man. He died to reconcile sinners to a holy God. *For unto us a child is born, unto us a son is given: and the government shall be upon his shoulder: and his name shall be called Wonderful, Counsellor, The mighty God, The everlasting Father,* **The Prince of Peace**. Isaiah 9:6

SON OF GOD - Jesus is the only begotten of the Father and is the Son of God. This is revealed throughout the New Testament. *And the angel answered and said unto her, The Holy Ghost shall come upon thee, and the power of the Highest shall overshadow thee: therefore also that holy thing shall be born of thee shall be called the* **Son of God**. *Also, For God so loved the world, that he gave his only begotten Son, that whosoever believeth in him should not perish, but have everlasting life; And we know that the* **Son of God** *is come, and hath given us an understanding, that we may know him that is true, and we are in him that is true, even in his Son Jesus Christ. This is the true God, and eternal life, Nathanael answered and saith unto him, Rabbi, thou art the* **Son of God**; *thou art the King of Israel. And, And the Word was made flesh, and dwelt among us, (and we beheld his glory, the glory as of the only begotten of the Father), full of grace and truth.* Luke 1:35; John 3:16; John 1:14; 1:49; 1 John 5:20

SON OF MAN - Son of God and Son of Man are personages of Jesus Christ. Son of Man affirms the humanity of Christ in His divinity as the Son of God. It depicts His all encompassing authority of man. *For the Father hath life in himself; so hath he given to the Son to have life in himself; And hath given him authority to execute judgment also, because he is the* **Son of man**. John 5:27

WORD - The Word is the second person, Jesus Christ, of the Trinity of God, who spoke all things out of nothing in the first Creation, who was in the beginning with God the Father, and was God, and by whom all things were created. *In the beginning was the* **Word**, *and the* **Word** *was with God, and the* **Word** *was God. Also, For there are three that bear record in heaven, the Father, the* **Word**, *and the Holy Ghost: and these three are one. And there are three that bear witness in earth, the Spirit, and the water, and the blood: and these three agree in one.* John 1:1; 1 John 5:7-8

WORD OF GOD – This is the name given to Christ that is unknown to all but Himself. It denotes the mystery of His divine person. *His eyes were as a flame of fire, and on his head were many crowns; and he had a name written, that no man knew, but he himself. And he was clothed with a vesture dipped in blood: and his name is called The* **Word of God**. Revelation 19:12-13

WORD OF LIFE – Jesus not only spoke words that would give us eternal life, but He is the very words of life. *That which was from the beginning, which we have heard, which we have seen with our eyes, which we have looked upon, and our hands have handled, of the* **Word of life**. 1 John 1:1

The Position of Christ

ALPHA AND OMEGA – We know God and Christ to be as One in the Trinity. God is Christ and Jesus is God. As One deity, they are the Alpha and Omega of all Creation. *I am the* **Alpha and Omega**, *the beginning and the end, saith the Lord, which is, and which was, and which is to come, the Almighty.* Also, *I am the* **Alpha and Omega**, *the beginning and the end, the first and the last.* And, *And he said unto me, It is done. I am* **Alpha and Omega**, *the beginning and the end, I will give unto him* *that is athirst of the fountain of the water of life freely.* Revelation 1:8; 22:13; 21:6

EMMANUEL – God came to earth in the second person of the Trinity, Christ, born of flesh to live among His people. *Behold, a virgin shall be with child, and shall bring forth a son, and they shall call his name* **Emmanuel***, which being interpreted is, God with us.* Matthew 1:23

I AM – We see the deity of God and Christ as One. Both God and Jesus declare to the people their omni-presence. *And God said unto Moses,* **I am** *that* **I am***: and he said, Thus shalt thou say unto the children of Israel,* **I am** *hath sent me unto you. Also, Jesus said unto them, Verily, verily, I say unto you, Before Abraham was,* **I am***.* Exodus 3:14; John 8:58

LORD OF ALL – Jesus is King over all things. The Father gave all Creation to His Son. *The word which God sent unto the children of Israel, preaching peace by Jesus Christ (he is* **Lord of all***:) That word, I say, ye know, which was published throughout all Judaea, and began from Galilee after the baptism which John preached; How God anointed Jesus of Nazareth with the Holy Ghost and with power: who went about doing good, and healing all that were oppressed of the devil; for God was with him.* Acts 10:36-38

TRUE GOD – God and Jesus are One Divinity, for God came to earth as Christ, and God is Jesus. In the personage of Christ, God reveals a part of His nature. *And we know that the Son of God is come, and hath given us an understanding, that we may know him that is true, and we are in him that is true, even in his Son Jesus*

*Christ. This is the **true God**, and eternal life.* 1 John 5:20

The Work of Christ

AUTHOR AND PERFECTER OF OUR FAITH - Eternal life is accomplished through the faith that is the gift of God, and Jesus is the founder of our faith and the finisher of it as well. From first to last, He is the source and sustainer of the faith that saves us. *Looking unto Jesus **the author and finisher of our faith**; who for the joy that was set before him endured the cross, despising the shame, and is set down at the right hand of the throne of God.* Also, *For by grace are ye saved through faith; and that not of yourselves: it is the gift of God. Not of works, lest any man should boast.* Hebrews 12:2; Ephesians 2:8-9

BREAD OF LIFE - Just as bread sustains life in the physical sense, Jesus is the bread that gives and sustains eternal life. God provided manna in the wilderness to feed His people, and He provided Jesus to give us eternal life through His body, broken for us. *And Jesus said unto them, I am the **bread of life,** he that cometh to me shall never hunger, and he that believeth on me shall never thirst.* Also, *I am the **bread of life**. Your fathers did eat manna in the wilderness, and are dead. This is the bread which cometh down from heaven, that a man may eat thereof, and not die. I am the living bread which came down from heaven: if any man eat of this bread, he shall live for ever: and the bread that I will give is my flesh, which I will give for the life of the world.* John 6:35; 48-51

BRIDEGROOM - Christ is the Bridegroom and the faithful saints are His bride. We are bound to Jesus in a covenant of grace that sets us apart as we wait for our Bridegroom to come for us. *And Jesus said unto them, Can the children of the bride chamber mourn, as long as the **bridegroom** is with them? But the days will come, when the **bridegroom** shall be taken from them, and then shall they fast. Also, Then shall the kingdom of heaven be likened unto ten virgins, which took their lamps, and went to meet the **bridegroom;** And at midnight there was a cry made, Behold, the **bridegroom** cometh; go ye out to meet him.* Matthew 9:15; 25:1; 25:6

DELIVERER - Just as the Israelites needed God to deliver them from bondage to Egypt, so Christ is our Deliverer from the bondage of sin. *And so all Israel shall be saved: as it is written, There shall come out of Sion the **Deliverer**, and shall turn away ungodliness from Jacob: For this is my covenant unto them, when I shall take away their sins.* Romans 11:26-27

GOOD SHEPHERD - A good shepherd is willing to risk his life to protect his sheep from predators. Jesus laid down His life for His sheep to gather us to Him in faith. He provides and protects us from worldly predators. *I am the **good shepherd**: for the **good shepherd** giveth his life for the sheep. Also, I am the **good shepherd**, and know my sheep, and am known of mine.* John 10:11; 10:14

HIGH PRIEST - The Jewish high priest entered the temple once a year to make atonement for the sins of the people. Jesus did this once for all at the Cross. *Wherefore, holy brethren, partakers of the heavenly calling,* *consider the Apostle and* **High Priest** *of our profession, Christ Jesus. Also, Seeing then that we have a great* **high priest***, that is passed into the heavens, Jesus the Son of God, let us hold fast our profession. And, For verily he took not on him the nature of angels; but he took on him the seed of Abraham. Wherefore in all things it behoved him to be made like unto his brethren, that he might be a merciful and faithful in things pertaining to God, to make a reconciliation for the sins of the people; Whither the forerunner is for us entered, even Jesus, made an* **high priest** *for ever after the order of Melchisedec.* Hebrews 3:1; 4:14; 2:16-17; 6:20

LAMB OF GOD – God's law called for the sacrifice of a spotless, unblemished lamb as an atonement for sin. Jesus became that lamb showing His patience in His sufferings and His readiness to die for His own. *The next day John seeth Jesus coming unto him, and saith, Behold the* **Lamb of God***, which taketh away the sin of the world. Also, And looking upon Jesus as he walked, he saith, Behold the* **Lamb of God.** John 1:29; 1:36

MEDIATOR – A mediator is one who goes between two parties to reconcile them. Christ is the one and only mediator who reconciles man to God. *For there is one God, and one* **mediator** *between God and men, the man Christ Jesus; Who gave himself a ransom for all to be testified in due time. Also, But now hath he obtained a more excellent ministry, by how much also he is the* **mediator** *of a better covenant, which was established upon better promises; For this cause he is the* **mediator** *of the new testament, that by means of death, for the redemption of the transgressions that were under the first testament, they which are called might receive the promises of* eternal inheritance; And to Jesus the **mediator** of the new covenant, and to the blood of sprinkling, that speaketh better things than that of Abel. 1 Timothy 2:5-6; Hebrews 8:8; 9:15; 12:24

ROCK - As life-giving water flowed from the rock Moses struck in the wilderness, Jesus is the Rock from which flows the living waters of eternal life. He is the Rock upon whom we build our spiritual house. *And did all drink the same spiritual drink: for they drank of that spiritual **Rock** that followed them: and that **Rock** is Christ.* 1 Corinthians 10:4

RESURRECTION AND LIFE - Jesus is the means to resurrect sinners to eternal life, just as He was resurrected from the grave. Our sin is buried with Him nailed at the Cross, and we are resurrected to walk in newness of life. *Jesus said unto her, I am the **resurrection, and the life**: he that believeth in me, though he were dead, yet shall he live.* Also, *And with great power gave the apostles witness of the resurrection of the Lord Jesus: and great grace was upon them all.* John 11:25; Acts 4:33

SAVIOUR - Jesus is Lord and Saviour. He saved His people by dying to redeem them, by giving the Holy Spirit to renew them by His power, by enabling them to overcome their spiritual enemies, by sustaining them in tribulation and in death, and by raising them up at the last day. *And she shall bring forth a son, and thou shalt call his name Jesus: for he shall save his people from their sins.* Also, *For unto you is born this day in the city of David a **Saviour**, which is Christ the Lord.* And, *Thou shalt also suck the milk of the Gentiles, and shalt suck the breast of kings: and thou shalt know that I the Lord am* thy **Saviour** and thy Redeemer, the mighty One of Jacob. Matthew 1:21; Luke 2:1; Isaiah 60:16

TRUE VINE – Jesus is the true vine who supplies to the branches (believer). Our life is in Christ, and He furnishes all we need in this lifetime and our new eternal life. *I am the **true vine**, and my Father is the husbandman.* John 15:1

WAY, TRUTH, LIFE – Jesus is our mediator and only path-way to the Father. There is no other means of securing a relationship with God and obtaining eternal life with the Father and His Son, but by Christ. *Jesus saith unto him, I am **the way, the truth, and the life**: no man cometh unto the Father, but by me.* John 14:6

NAMES OF JESUS CHRIST

There are over two hundred names in the Bible for Jesus Christ. The specific names depicts that everything God spoke was manifested by the *Word* at Creation and fulfilled by Christ on the Cross. He is the Son of God and Son of Man. Throughout the generations spanning six thousand years, the Scriptures reflect the life of Christ.

It has always been about the Son of God when He was worshipped as *a shadow of things to come* in the Old Testament, to His time on Earth referenced in the New Testament, to His death and resurrection on the Cross at Golgotha. There will be a second appearance on Earth, for our King is returning to take us home.

ADAM: *And so it is written, The first man **Adam** was made a living soul; the last **Adam** was made a quickening spirit.* 1 Corinthians 15:45

ADVOCATE: *My little children, these things write I unto you, that ye sin not. And if any man sin, we have an **advocate** with the Father, Jesus Christ the righteous.* 1 John 2:1

ALMIGHTY: *I am Alpha and Omega, the beginning and the ending, saith the Lord, which is, and which was, and which is to come, the **Almighty**.* Revelation 1:8

ALPHA AND OMEGA: *I am **Alpha** and **Omega**, the beginning and the ending, saith the Lord, which is, and which was, and which is to come, the Almighty.* Revelation 1:8

AMEN: *And unto the angel of the church of the Laodiceans write; These things saith the **Amen**, the faithful and true witness, the beginning of the creation of God.* Revelation 3:14

APOSTLE OF OUR PROFESSION: *Wherefore, holy brethren, partakers of the heavenly calling, consider the **Apostle** and High Priest **of our profession**, Christ Jesus.* Hebrews 3:1

ARM OF THE LORD: *Awake, awake, put on strength, O **arm of the Lord**; awake, as in the ancient days, in the generations of old. Art thou not it that hath cut Rahab, and wounded the dragon? Who hath believed our report? And to whom is the arm of the Lord revealed?* Isaiah 53:1; and Isaiah 51: 9

AUTHOR AND FINISHER OF OUR FAITH: *Looking unto Jesus **the author and finisher of our faith**; who for the joy that was set before him endured the cross, despising the shame, and is set down at the right hand of the throne of God.* Hebrews 12:2

AUTHOR OF ETERNAL SALVATION: *And being made perfect, he became the **author of eternal salvation** unto all them that obey him.* Hebrews 5:9

BEGINNING OF CREATION OF GOD: *And unto the angel of the church of the Laodiceans write; These things saith the Amen, the faithful and true witness, the **beginning of the creation of God**.* Revelation 3:14

BELOVED SON: *Behold my servant, whom I have chosen; my **beloved**, in whom my soul is well pleased: I will put my spirit upon him, and he shall show judgment to the Gentiles.* Matthew 12:18

BLESSED AND ONLY POTENTATE: *Which in his times he shall show, who is the **blessed and only Potentate**, the King of kings, and Lord of lords.* 1 Timothy 6:15

BRANCH: *In that day shall the **branch** of the Lord be beautiful and glorious, and the fruit of the earth shall be excellent and comely for them that are escaped of Israel.* Isaiah 4:2

BREAD OF LIFE FROM HEAVEN: *Then Jesus said unto them, Verily, verily, I say unto you, Moses gave you not that **bread from heaven**; but my Father giveth you the true **bread from heaven**.* John 6:32

CAPTAIN OF SALVATION: *For it became him, for whom are all things, and by whom are all things, in bringing many sons unto glory, to make the **captain of their salvation** perfect through sufferings.* Hebrews 2:10

CHIEF SHEPHERD: *And when the **chief Shepherd** shall appear, ye shall receive a crown of glory that fadeth not away.* 1 Peter 5:4

CHRIST OF GOD: *He said unto them, But whom say ye that I am? Peter answering said, The **Christ of God**.* Luke 9:20

CONSOLATION OF ISRAEL: *And, behold, there was a man in Jerusalem, whose name was Simeon; and the same man was just and devout, waiting for the **consolation of Israel**: and the Holy Ghost was upon him.* Luke 2:25

CHIEF CORNERSTONE: *The stone which the builders refused is become the head stone of the corner. And are built upon the foundation of the apostles and prophets, Jesus Christ himself being the **chief corner stone**; In who all the building fitly framed together groweth unto a holy temple in the Lord.* Psalm 118:22; Ephesians 2:20-21

COUNSELLOR: *For unto us a child is born, unto us a son is given: and the government shall be upon his shoulder: and his name shall be called Wonderful, **Counsellor**, The Mighty God, The Everlasting Father, The Prince of Peace.* Isaiah 9:6

CREATOR: *All things were made by him; and without him was not any thing made that was made. Who is the image of the invisible God, the firstborn of every creature: For by him were all things **created**, that are in heaven, and that are in earth, visible and invisible, whether they be thrones, or dominions, or principalities, or powers: all things were **created** by him, and for him: and he is before all things, and by all things consist.* Colossians 1:15-16; John 1:3

DAYSPRING: *Through the tender mercy of our God; whereby the **dayspring** from on high hath visited us.* Luke 1:78

DELIVERER: *And so all Israel shall be saved: as it is written, There shall come out of Sion the **Deliverer**, and shall turn away ungodliness from Jacob.* Romans 11:26

DESIRE OF THE NATIONS: *And I will shake all nations, and the **desire of all nations** shall come: and I will fill this house with glory, saith the Lord of hosts.* Haggai 2:7

DOOR: *Then said Jesus unto them again, Verily, verily, I say unto you, I am the **door** of the sheep.* John 10:7

ELECT OF GOD: *Behold my servant, whom I uphold; **mine elect**, in whom my soul delighteth; I have put my spirit upon him: he shall bring forth judgment to the Gentiles.* Isaiah 42:1

EVERLASTING FATHER: *For unto us a child is born, unto us a son is given: and the government shall be upon his shoulder: and his name shall be called Wonderful, Counsellor, The Mighty God, The **Everlasting Father**, The Prince of Peace.* Isaiah 9:6

FAITHFUL WITNESS: *And from Jesus Christ, who is the **faithful witness**, and the first begotten of the dead, and the prince of the kings of the earth. Unto him that loved us, and washed us from our sins in his own blood.* Revelation 1:5

FIRST AND LAST: *And when I saw him, I fell at his feet as* dead. And he laid his right hand upon me, saying unto me, Fear not; I am the **first and the last**. Revelation 1:17

FIRST BEGOTTEN: *And from Jesus Christ, who is the faithful witness, and the **first begotten** of the dead, and the prince of the kings of the earth. Unto him that loved us, and washed us from our sins in his own blood.* Revelation 1:5

FORERUNNER: *Whither the **forerunner** is for us entered, even Jesus, made an high priest forever after the order of Melchisedec.* Hebrews 6:20

GLORY OF THE LORD: *And the **glory of the Lord** shall be revealed, and all flesh shall see it together: for the mouth of the Lord hath spoken it.* Isaiah 40:5

GOD: *The voice of him that crieth in the wilderness, Prepare ye the way of the Lord, make straight in the desert a highway for our **God**.* Isaiah 40: 3

GOD BLESSED: *Whose are the fathers, and of whom as concerning the flesh Christ came, who is over all, **God blessed** forever. Amen.* Romans 9:5

GOOD SHEPHERD: *I am the **good shepherd**: the **good shepherd** giveth his life for the sheep.* John 10:11

GOVERNOR: *And thou Bethlehem, in the land of Juda, art not the least among the princes of Juda: for out of thee shall come a **Governor**, that shall rule my people Israel.* Matthew 2:6

GREAT HIGH PRIEST: *Seeing then that we have a **great high priest**, that is passed into the heavens, Jesus the Son of God, let us hold fast our profession.* Hebrews 4:14

HEAD OF THE CHURCH: *And hath put all things under his feet, and gave him to be the **head over all things to the church**.* Ephesians 1:22

HEIR OF ALL THINGS: *Hath in these last days spoken unto us by his Son, whom he hath appointed **heir of all things**, by whom also he made the worlds.* Hebrews 1:2

HOLY CHILD: *For of a truth against thy **holy child** Jesus, whom thou hast anointed, both Herod, and Pontius Pilate, with the Gentiles, and the people of Israel, were gathered together.* Acts 4:27

HOLY ONE: *But ye denied the **Holy One** and the Just, and desired a murderer to be granted unto you.* Acts 3:14

HOLY ONE OF GOD: *Saying, Let us alone; what have we to do with thee, thou Jesus of Nazareth? Art thou come to destroy us? I know thee who thou art, the **Holy One of God**.* Mark 1:24

HOLY ONE OF ISRAEL: *Fear not, thou worm Jacob, and ye men of Israel; I will help thee, saith the Lord, and thy redeemer, the **Holy One of Israel**.* Isaiah 41:14

HORN OF SALVATION: *And hath raised up an **horn of salvation** for us in the house of his servant David.* Luke 1:69

I AM: *Jesus said unto them, Verily, verily, I say unto you, Before Abraham was, **I am**.* John 8:58

IMAGE OF GOD: *In whom the god of this world hath blinded the minds of them which believe not, lest the light of the glorious gospel of Christ, who is the **image of God**, should shine unto them.* 2 Corinthians 4:4

IMMANUEL: *Therefore the Lord himself shall give you a sign; Behold, a virgin shall conceive, and bear a son, and shall call his name **Immanuel**.* Isaiah 7:14

JEHOVAH: *Trust ye in the Lord for ever: for in the Lord **Jehovah** is everlasting strength.* Isaiah 26:4

JESUS: *And she shall bring forth a son, and thou shalt call his name **Jesus** for he shall save his people from their sins.* Matthew 1:21

JESUS OF NAZARETH: *And the multitude said, This is **Jesus** the prophet **of Nazareth** of Galilee.* Matthew 21:11

JUDGE OF ISRAEL: *Now gather thyself in troops, O daughter of troops: he hath laid siege against us: they shall smite the **judge of Israel** with a rod upon the cheek.* Micah 5:1

THE JUST ONE: *Which of the prophets have not your fathers persecuted? And they have slain them which showed before of the coming of the **Just One**; of whom ye have been now the betrayers and murderers.* Acts 7:52

KING: *Rejoice greatly, O daughter of Zion; shout, O daughter of Jerusalem: behold, thy **King** cometh unto thee: he is just, and having salvation; lowly, and riding upon an ass, and upon a colt the foal of an ass.* Zechariah 9:9

KING OF THE AGES: *Now unto the **King eternal**, immortal, invisible, the only wise God, be honour and glory for ever and ever. Amen.* 1 Timothy 1:17

KING OF THE JEWS: *Saying, Where is he that is born **King of the Jews**? For we have seen his star in the east, and are come to worship him.* Matthew 2:2

KING OF KINGS: *Which in his times he shall show, who is the blessed and only Potentate, the **King of kings**, and Lord of lords.* 1 Timothy 6:15

KING OF SAINTS: *And they sing the song of Moses the servant of God, and the song of the Lamb, saying, Great and marvelous are thy works, Lord God Almighty; just and true are thy ways, thou **King of saints**.* Revelation 15:3

LAWGIVER: *For the Lord is our judge, the Lord is our **lawgiver**, the Lord is our king; he will save us.* Isaiah 33:22

LAMB: *And all that dwell upon the earth shall worship him, whose names are not written in the book of life of the **Lamb** slain from the foundation of the world.* Revelation 13:8

LAMB OF GOD: *The next day John seeth Jesus coming unto him, and saith, Behold the **Lamb of God**, which taketh away the sin of the world.* John 1:29

LEADER AND COMMANDER: *Behold, I have given him for a witness to the people, a **leader and commander** to the people.* Isaiah 55:4

THE LIFE: *Jesus saith unto him, I am the way, the truth, and **the life**: no man cometh unto the Father, but by me.* John 14:6

LIGHT OF THE WORLD: *Then spake Jesus again unto them, saying, I am the **light of the world**: he that followeth me shall not walk in darkness, but shall have the light of life.* John 8:12

LION OF THE TRIBE OF JUDAH: *And one of the elders saith unto me, Weep not: behold, the **Lion of the tribe of Juda**, the Root of David, hath prevailed to open the book, and to loose the seven seals thereof.* Revelation 5:5

LORD OF ALL: *The word which God sent unto the children of Israel, preaching peace by Jesus Christ: (he is **Lord of all**).* Acts 10:36

LORD OF GLORY: *Which none of the princes of this world knew: for had they known it, they would not have crucified the **Lord of glory**.* 1 Corinthians 2:8

LORD OF LORDS: *Which in his times he shall show, who is the blessed and only Potentate, the King of kings, and*

Lord of lords. 1 Timothy 6:15

LORD OF OUR RIGHTEOUSNESS: *In this days Judah shall be saved, and Israel shall dwell safely: and this is his name whereby he shall be called, The **Lord our Righteousness**. Jeremiah 23:6*

MAN OF SORROWS: *He is despised and rejected of men; a **man of sorrows**, and acquainted with grief: and we hid as it were our faces from him; he was despised, and we esteemed him not. Isaiah 53:3*

MEDIATOR: *For there is one God, and one **mediator** between God and men, the man Christ Jesus. 1 Timothy 2:5*

MESSENGER OF THE COVENANT: *Behold, I will send my messenger, and he shall prepare the way before me: and the Lord, whom ye seek, shall suddenly come to his temple, even the **messenger of the covenant**, whom ye delight in: behold, he shall come, saith the Lord of hosts. Malachi 3:1*

MESSIAH: *Know therefore and understand, that from the going forth of the commandment to restore and to build Jerusalem unto the **Messiah** the Prince shall be seven weeks, and threescore and two weeks: the street shall be built again, and the wall, even in troublous times. Daniel 9:26 He first findeth his own brother Simon, and saith unto him, We have found the **Messiah**, which is, being interpreted, the Christ. John 1:41*

MIGHTY GOD: *For unto us a child is born, unto us a son is given: and the government shall be upon his shoulder:*

and his name shall be called Wonderful, Counsellor, The **Mighty God**, The Everlasting Father, The Prince of Peace. Isaiah 9:6

MIGHTY ONE: *Thou shalt also suck the milk of the Gentiles, and shalt suck the breast of kings: and thou shalt know that I the Lord am thy Saviour and thy Re-deemer, the **mighty One** of Jacob.* Isaiah 60:16

MORNING STAR: *I Jesus have sent mine angel to testify unto you these things in the churches. I am the root and the offspring of David, and the bright and **morning star**.* Revelation 22:16

NAZARENE: *And he came and dwelt in a city called **Nazareth**: that it might be fulfilled which was spoken by the prophets, He shall be called a **Nazarene**.* Matthew 2:23

ONLY BEGOTTEN SON: *No man hath seen God at any time; the **only begotten Son**, which is in the bosom of the Father, he hath declared him.* John 1:18

OUR PASSOVER: *Purge out therefore the old leaven, that ye may be a new lump, as ye are unleavened. For even Christ **our passover** is sacrificed for us.* 1 Corinthians 5:7

PRINCE OF LIFE: *And killed the **Prince of life**, whom God hath raised from the dead; whereof we are witnesses.* Acts 3:15

PRINCE OF KINGS: *And from Jesus Christ, who is the faithful witness, and the first begotten of the dead, and the **prince of the kings** of the earth. Unto him that loved us, and washed us from our sins in his own blood.* Revelation 1:5

PRINCE OF PEACE: *For unto us a child is born, unto us a son is given: and the government shall be upon his shoulder: and his name shall be called Wonderful, Counsellor, The Mighty God, The Everlasting Father, The **Prince of Peace**.* Isaiah 9:6

PROPHET: *And he said unto them, What things? And they said unto him, Concerning Jesus of Nazareth, which was a **prophet** mighty in deed and word before God and all the people. For Moses truly said unto the fathers, A **prophet** shall the Lord your God raise up unto you of your brethren, like unto me; him shall ye hear in all things whatsoever he shall say unto you.* Acts 3:22; Luke 24:19

REDEEMER: *For I know that my **redeemer** liveth, and that he shall stand at the latter day upon the earth.* Job 19:25

RESURRECTION AND LIFE: *Jesus said unto her, I am the **resurrection and the life**: he that believeth in me, though he were dead, yet shall he live.* John 11:25

ROCK: *And did all drink the same spiritual drink: for they drank of that spiritual **Rock** that followed them: and that **Rock** was Christ.* 1 Corinthians 10:4

ROOT OF DAVID: *I Jesus have sent mine angel to testify* unto you these things in the churches. I am the **root** and the offspring **of David**, and the bright and morning star. Revelation 22:16

ROSE OF SHARON: *I am the **rose of Sharon**, and the lily of the valleys. Solomon 2:1*

SAVIOUR: *For unto you is born this day in the city of David a **Saviour**, which is Christ the Lord. Luke 2:1*

SEED OF WOMAN: *And I will put enmity between thee and the woman, and between thy seed and **her seed**; it shall bruise thy head, and thou shalt bruise his heel. Genesis 3:15*

SHEPHERD AND BISHOP OF SOULS: *For ye were as sheep going astray; but are now returned unto the **Shepherd and Bishop of your souls**. 1 Peter 2:25*

SHILOH: *The scepter shall not depart from Judah, nor a lawgiver from between his feet, until **Shiloh** come; and unto him shall the gathering of the people be. Genesis 49:10*

SON OF THE BLESSED: *But he held his peace, and answered nothing. Again the high priest asked him, and said unto him, Art thou the Christ, the **Son of the Blessed**. Mark 14:61*

SON OF DAVID: *The book of the generation of Jesus Christ, the **son of David**, the son of Abraham. Matthew 1:1*

SON OF GOD: And was there until the death of Herod: that it might be fulfilled which was spoken of the Lord by prophet, saying, Out of Egypt have I called **my son**. Matt-hew 2:15

SON OF THE HIGHEST: He shall be great, and shall be called the **Son of the Highest**: and the Lord God shall give unto him the throne of his father David. Luke 1:32

SUN OF RIGHTEOUSNESS: But unto you that fear my name shall the **Sun of Righteousness** arise with healing in his wings; and ye shall go forth, and grow up as calves of the stall. Malachi 4:2

TRUE LIGHT: That was the **true Light**, which lighteth every man that cometh into the world. John 1:9

TRUE VINE: I am the **true vine**, and my Father is the husbandman. John 15:1

TRUTH: And the Word was made flesh, and dwelt among us, (and we beheld his glory, the glory as of the only begotten of the Father,) full of grace and **truth**. John 1:14

WITNESS: Behold, I have given him for a **witness** to the people a leader and commander to the people. Isaiah 55:4

WORD: In the beginning was the **Word**, and the **Word** was with God, and the **Word** was God. John 1:1

WORD OF GOD: *And he was clothed with a vesture dipped in blood: and his name is called The **Word of God.*** Revelation 19:13

ADDITIONAL

BOOK EXCERPTS

Fervent Prayer

EXCERPT

Fervent Prayer gives insight to the most frequently asked question among Christians today. When we pray and an answer doesn't seem to be forthcoming, what has happened? Rather than accept a humanistic inclination that God is withholding; perhaps, we should turn inward to search the answer. Are we unknowingly blocking His supernatural power from entering our earthen circumstance? God does not withhold His blessings from His children, but has given the keys to His Kingdom to unlock heavenly treasures and receive His promises. *And I will give unto you the keys of the kingdom of heaven: and whatsoever thou shalt bind on earth shall be bound in heaven: and whatsoever thou shalt loose on earth shall be loosed in heaven.* Matthew 16:19

    Our heavenly Father knows of our prayer before we utter the first word; therefore, praying is for our benefit showing our position of faith and trust, whereby the one *fervent prayer* releases Kingdom power. Though righteous in Christ, are we sabotaging our relationship with God? Is our faith based on the law or grace? Is our belief tainted with unbelief? Is our communication a pleading prayer, or one of thanksgiving and praise knowing our answer is provided? These are some of the questions that are answered in *Fervent Prayer*. In revealing the hinderances that can obstruct receiving, we witness the power of a *fervent prayer*.

> *The effectual fervent prayer of a*
> *righteous man availeth much.*
> James 5:16

Children in the Crossfire

EXCERPT

Children in the Crossfire reveals the ongoing warfare between Lucifer and God which began before there was man. When you study the events in biblical history as a snapshot of sequential scenes, it exposes what transpired in the Kingdom of Heaven and continues in the Kingdom of Earth.

It all began with Lucifer's defiance and attempt to oust the Almighty King from His throne. Lucifer was evicted, along with the fallen angels, to the Kingdom of Earth. Realizing he wasn't going to be the king of Heaven, he set his objective to be king of Earth and stole the position from Adam through deceit. Satan rules this earthen Kingdom with the same measure of deception and your spiritual death is his desire, for it is the spirit person, born in Christ, that makes you a child of the Almighty King. We are all the target as he continuously attempts to derail us from the truth of our Most High God.

The spiritual battle is presently and actively ongoing behind the scenes in your life, and unbeknownst, playing havoc in your daily affairs. Most often when matters in life are array, we have a tendency to fault our heavenly Father. However, it isn't God but Satan, the god of this earthen Kingdom, who rules with intent to steal, kill, and destroy. Understanding this spiritual battle will enable you to deflect and denounce his attempts to place obstacles in your life.

Your stronghold in this spiritual battle is to put on the armor of God with His hedge of protection and be enveloped in your Father's arms. Be guarded and protected by the One who gives you life, loves you, desires for you to be His child, and who will give you eternity in His Kingdom. With your gift of a free will, choose the Almighty King of the Kingdom of Heaven and be released from the entrapments of this earthen ruler, so that you will no longer be a child caught in the crossfire.

Everlasting Love, God's Greatest Gift

EXCERPT

Everlasting Love, God's Greatest Gift reveals the love of the Father for His children. From the beginning of Creation, God fashioned the heavens and the earth for you with an enduring and *everlasting love*, never forgotten or forsaken. Mercy, grace, faith, blessings, promises, gifts, and supernatural power abound to the faithful children of the Almighty King. We are sons and daughters, heirs in Christ within the Kingdom of Heaven with the privilege to come before the throne of our Lord.

Everlasting Love, God's Greatest Gift presents an intimate journey into the trinity of God as the Father, the Son, and the Holy Ghost; the trinity of man created with a spirit, soul, and body; and the Kingdom of Heaven which functions with mercy, grace, and faith.

We obtain a life-altering makeover through the blood of Christ and given the gift of faith to unlock the mysteries of God's Kingdom that we may obtain His dunamis power to defeat fear, anxiety, depression, confusion, illness, disease, heartache, financial disparity, and addictions. God intends for His children to overcome and triumph in any adversity and be set free from whatever holds you captive as the result of living in a fallen world.

Take the key of faith, place it in the Kingdom lock, and turn to the truth in His Word to open a new beginning in your life today. Live as a rightful heir of the Almighty King of the Kingdom of Heaven, secure and sealed in the Father's *Everlasting Love*.

This book includes a study guide beneficial for individual or group participation. In addition, spirit topics are included with a comprehensive look at the nature, works, and position of the Son of God in the trinity of the Father, the Son, and the Holy Ghost.

ABOUT THE AUTHOR

Patricia Marlett is dedicated to writing inspirational novels for both the adult and young reader genres. With a contemporary platform, she enjoys penning plots that reflect life experiences through drama, intrigue, suspense, humor, and love. Inspirational messages are subtly woven within the endearing themes of her stories lending to heartfelt expressions from laughter to tears and always with hope and joy.

Patricia's non-fiction titles exemplifies her desire to reveal the Word of God that all may want to know their Lord and Savior through a personal relationship with Christ.

Visit Patricia at her website, www.patriciamarlett.com, to learn of her passion for writing, view her books, and for contact information.

www.ingramcontent.com/pod-product-compliance
Lightning Source LLC
Chambersburg PA
CBHW071723040426
42446CB00011B/2194